GOOD MORNING
GOD

21-day devotional to help jump-start your day

T KING

Amanda Williams, T Bacon

TJ&M Publishing LTD CO

Dedicated to the one my heart loves.
Song of Solomon 3:4

GOOD MORNING GOD

ISBN: 978-0-578-36659-3

Cover Design by T Bacon
Edited by Amanda Williams

readwithme@tjmpublishing.com

Contents

Stay out of it

Read; John 4

What an odd message to jump-start your day with. Although the message may seem strange, I promise it will make sense in a minute. As Christians, it is imperative that we know *and* understand that we do not have to be involved in everything. Sometimes we can find ourselves running to the scene of a crime when all that is required are our prayers. When things go wrong with the people around us, it is not always our job to show up and attempt to make things better. We have to know when to stay and when to go. The thing that I love about God, is even when we try to insert ourselves, he moves us right out of the way. Our presence could very well be a hindrance to a situation, as opposed to being a source of help.

In John 4, we can clearly see that Jesus traveled to Samaria and met the woman at the well alone. The disciples would have gotten in the way. This woman was considered to be the lowest of the low, not only because she was a Samaritan, but also because she was a woman who was considered to be only an item. Traditionally, her race was despised by the Jews. Think about it, how would the conversation go if the disciples were present? Would she have even approached them? Would the disciples have rejected her? I believe that Jesus ordained this holy encounter just the way it was because the disciples would not have been able to put their traditional views aside at the time, in order for this woman to get the word that she needed.

Let's think about ourselves in this instance. Have there been moments where you were unable to put your feelings aside for the greater good and truly see God in the middle of a situation? It is times like these when we really need to be tuned in with God so that we know when to show up, or when to fall back. It is my prayer that my presence is never a hindrance to what God is doing, but if my very presence will oppose the work of the Lord, then I pray that I am Christian enough to fall back and send a prayer that will go places that I am not authorized in the spirit to go.

Pray with me:

Lord, I thank you for this day. I ask that you forgive me for my sins, those that I know of and those that I do not. Father, I pray that I am able to hear what the spirit is saying to me concerning the places I should tread. Lord, I ask that you always order my steps and guide me to where it is that you want me to go. I pray, my heavenly father, that my presence will never be a hindrance, but Lord if it is, I ask that you, one; do a work in me, and two; send someone in my place that is able to get done what you need to get done for the glorification of your kingdom. I thank you that you have heard my prayer and I ask that you continue to do work in me. I am a willing vessel. I pray all these things in Jesus' name, AMEN.

Good morning God activity page

What have you learned?

Has a situation ever occurred where you inserted yourself and make it worse? If so, what?

What did you take away from that encounter?

Identifying all of me

Read; Psalm 139:23-24

Did you know that there are four parts of self? The first part is our "open self". This is the part of us that we share with others. The things that we would like other people to know, whether it be through our actions or our words. Open self is an open book. The next self is the "hidden self". This part, clearly, is the part of us that is unknown to others, even those who are closest to us. Let's be real, there are some things about ourselves that we prefer that no one knows about. Next, we have "blind self". This one is pretty interesting. This part of ourselves is the part that we don't know, but others do. All of us have triggers, ways, attitudes, and routines that we have become blind to and do not even notice that we do them, but others see them clearly. This part of ourselves is the part where denial can rest. The final part of self is; "unknown self". This is the part that is *most* interesting. This part of us is information that is not known by us or by others. Only God knows. I love the fact that God knows me more than anybody in this entire world, including myself. Not only does he know me, but he chooses to actively love me despite all of my hang-ups. When we feel like we are least deserving, God is there, because he sees around the corner, when we can only see to the corner. When we see no way out, God has already *made* a way out. I appreciate the fact that when someone else may see a big mess, God sees a wonderfully hand-crafted masterpiece designed by the master himself.

This scripture is simply asking God to search us. Since he knows us better than anybody, he also knows the things that do not belong. Did you know that we can be unaware of things in our lives that do not belong? But God! He's aware of it all and this scripture in verse 24 makes it clear that God has the ability to search and examine us, but it doesn't just stop there. Not only will he examine us, but he is also able to lead us away from these things and into everlasting. Doing what is right, leads to the everlasting. Following God's commands, leads to the everlasting. Meditate on these scriptures throughout the day when things arise in you. Ask God to examine you and lead you to a place where all the parts of you are acceptable in his sight.

Pray with me:

Lord, I thank you for this day. I ask that you forgive me for my sins, those that I know of and those that I do not. I thank you that you know and love all of me. Father, I ask that you examine my heart, and if there be anything in there that is not like you, I ask that you remove it. I don't want to be hindered by anything that will keep me from fully getting what you have for me. Guide me today, help me to make wise decisions, so that when others see me, they are really seeing a reflection of you. I give you all the honor and the praise, and I thank you in advance for hearing my prayer. In the mighty name of your son Jesus, AMEN.

Good morning God activity page

What have you learned?

Which of the four parts to self stick out to you the most? Why?

Can you identify the adjustments that need to be made in your life? What are they?

Right where I am

Read; Philippians 4:11

It took me a long time to accept the path that God had for me. I spent years living this life in God, but I was not really happy with where I was (because of my own decisions) and definitely not happy with the hard lessons that I had to learn. In my adolescent years, I had a pretty carefree life. There were things that I went through, but for the most part, my childhood was a good one. I came from a two-parent home, and both my mother and father worked. Also, as far as I knew, we were pretty good financially. Fast forward to the tender age of 19. There I was, married with a family and we were struggling. It was hard. I never had to figure out how to handle money until I moved out from under the shelter of my parents. I never even gave paying bills and running a home one thought. God taught us many lessons in the beginning, but the hardest lesson to learn was to be content with where I was at that time. Most importantly, he taught me to be content with the things that I couldn't change.

There are a lot of people that are not happy with where they are in life, however, you have to gauge *why* you are where you are in life. It has to be understood that; those things that I can change to make my life better, I need to do. However, those things that I cannot change to make my life more pleasurable, I have to learn this dirty word called...contentment. Now, my husband and I can say that we weathered the storm. These storms strengthened our faith and taught us to truly depend on him and each other. No longer do I have to live through someone else's testimony. I know for a fact what the master can do! If you would have told us back then, that we would become entrepreneurs, I wouldn't have believed it. God is faithful. And the blessings just keep coming!

In the book of Philippians, Paul writes this joyous letter to the church. The words that he wrote were so good, that he needed to let them know that he was not writing the letter to get anything out of them because he had learned to be content in whatever state that he was in. At the time, he was in prison. We could all take a page from Paul and learn that whatever and wherever we are in life, we have to be ok with what God is doing. If I say I trust God, then I have to trust the process and be content with where he has me. ASK God to help you trust his process and to give you peaceful happiness with the current state that you are in, KNOWING that trouble doesn't always last.

Pray with me:

Lord, I thank you for this day. I ask that you forgive me for my sins, those that I know of and those that I do not. Father, I thank you that you are aware of where I am in life and you are also aware of all of the things that I want out of life. I ask that you give me patience and help me be content with where you have me right now. There is something you want me to learn, and father I am willing to learn that lesson in order to go where you will have me to. Thank you, God, for your love and your perfect guidance and I thank you in advance for hearing my prayer. In Jesus' name, AMEN.

Good morning God activity page

What have you learned?

Is being content with where you are and what you have a challenge? If so, why?

What are things that you can do on your own to change your circumstances? What do you need God to do?

This can't wait

Read; Luke 8:40-56

Have you ever had a need that you felt was so urgent that you needed God to do something right away? I know I have. I wanted God to do quite a few things right away in my life. Sometimes he did, and sometimes he didn't. The times when he didn't do it right away, I pouted a bit, and when he finally did it, I was grateful that he chose to do it in his timing and not mine. To us, we feel like he is waiting, but I believe, to God, he is just simply following his plan. God doesn't work in delays; we only see them as delays because they are not done when we feel they should be done. God simply works in his timing.

This scripture talks about Jesus, the woman with the issue of blood, and Jairus (the ruler of the synagogue). While Jesus was making his way through the crowd Jairus approached him because he had a need, and it was a matter of life and death. On the way to Jairus' house, Jesus was touched by the woman with the issue of blood and he took the time to take care of her needs first while Jairus' situation was "put on pause". While Jesus was dealing with her, Jairus' situation took a turn and it seemed like it was too late, but Jesus told Jairus to believe. Fast forward, Jairus got just what he was looking for when Jesus arrived on the scene, and his problem was no longer a problem. Do you think he complained about waiting for it? Remember that God's timing is not ours and he knows very well what we are in need of. Nothing takes him by surprise. Trusting God means that you trust him to do his work when he sees fit and not when we would like him to.

Pray with me:

Lord, I thank you for this day. I ask that you forgive me for my sins, those that I know of and those that I do not. I am coming to you today, asking for peace with your timing. Father, I know that you know just what I need and I also know that you will give it to me when you are ready. Help me to have peace with what you have for me and when you have it for me. I thank you in advance for hearing my prayer. In Jesus' name, AMEN.

Good morning God activity page

What have you learned?

What is something that you are wanting God to do for you right now?

What are some ways that you can patiently wait on the Lord until he moves on your behalf?

Spiritual Vision

Read; 1 Kings 17: 1-16

I was watching television the other day. You know, one of those nature shows. It actually interests my husband and one of my daughters more than it interests the rest of us, but this particular segment stuck out to me. The narrator was going on about the Chital deer. Did you know that this particular type of deer only has two types of color receptors? They are blind to red and orange. So, when their enemy, a tiger, is present, they are vulnerable because they cannot see the orange coloring of the tiger. It is nearly impossible for them to register that the enemy is nearby. They are not, however, entirely defenseless. The Langur money is known to be "the eyes of the forest". They have three types of color receptors and can see as humans do. They are the alarm system for the deer to alert them of danger.

While watching this program, I was reminded of the woman in 1 Kings 17 who Elijah approached. In verse 11 he told her to go and get him a morsel of bread. She responded and told him that she only had a handful of meal and a little oil. She was already of the mindset that she and her son would starve to death and she had already begun to prepare for it. Elijah, however, told her to fear not and to go and do what he had said. If you are reading the scriptures provided, then you already know the outcome of the story, but I bet you are wondering why in the world did this particular biblical encounter remind me of the show I watched on television? It reminded me of a phrase that my husband often uses when he preaches. He says; "we only see *to* the corner, but God sees *around* the corner". In nature, you have this animal with this vision problem and is having a hard time not becoming prey, but God placed a monkey to be its eyes. *I* only saw that this animal will surely die. My mind did not even register that God would make a way, even for this animal. Don't we do that with life as well? When there is danger or a problem ahead, we can only see what's staring us right in the face and can't see any further than the situation. God, however, sees us overcoming the problem, and living in victory. In this scenario, Elijah acts as the Langur Monkey does. In a way, he sounded the alarm to this woman's inner self and told her to fear not. I love the fact that even when she told him of her situation, he told her to do as he said and because she chose to adhere to the man of God, she and her son were blessed beyond measure.

I thank God that his vision reaches further than mine and anyone else's can. He is so meticulous and calculated with the details of our lives. How can we not love him? How can we not spend time with someone who goes to such great lengths to do the things that he does? Our prayer today should be that God helps us with our spiritual vision. That he enlightens us of the things around us or sends someone to enlighten us and help us with the dangers around. Just like Elijah helped this woman see that she and her son would live, and not die.

Pray with me:

Lord, I thank you for this day. I ask that you forgive me for my sins, those that I know of and those that I do not. God, you are so good, and you are so calculated. I want to give you praise today for the lengths that you go to protect me. When the enemy is around, you send something or someone to sound the alarm and get me out of harm's way. I am forever grateful for all of the things you have shielded me from and will continue to shield me from. I also ask that you sharpen my spiritual vision, that I may see a camouflaged enemy. I thank you in advance for hearing my prayer. In Jesus' name, AMEN.

Good morning God activity page

What have you learned?

_____
_____
_____
_____
_____
_____
_____
_____
_____
_____

What are some things that God used others to protect you from?

_____
_____
_____
_____
_____
_____
_____
_____
_____
_____

Have you ever been the "spiritual eyes" for someone else? If so, what did you do?

_____
_____
_____
_____
_____

Prayer is life

Read; Matt 14:23; Mark 1:35; Luke 9:18; John 12:27-30

How often do you pray? Is it a priority in your life? Do you do it every day or is it put on the back burner? I think you would be surprised to know the number of Christians that do not take the time to have a conversation with God. The times 8 am, 12 pm, and 9 pm have played a humongous role in my life and in the lives of those that are connected to our ministry. My pastor, who also happens to be my husband, was directed by God years ago, to teach the importance of having a connection with God. What is the best way to connect with him? Through prayer. 8 am, 12 pm, and 9 pm are the times that each one of us in the ministry takes the time to pray. I always love when we are all together for one reason or another and all of our alarms go off at the same time. Even after all these years, our alarms are still set to these times. There have been a few instances when I was somewhere with someone not a part of the ministry and my alarm went off. I would take the time to explain the alarm and let them know that I was about to pray. 100% of the time, the individual wanted to be included. Now I am not telling you to set an alarm to pray each day, but I will encourage you to if you are not talking to God on a regular basis and maybe need a little help. After a while, it becomes second nature. Even my children know what the times are and often pray with us when the alarms sound.

There are so many scriptures in the bible that depict Christ praying. I only chose a few for time's sake, but you can always go back and take a look at all of the times when Jesus was in prayer. I chose this subject, for this day, because I wanted to highlight the importance of prayer and talking with God. Praying is so important that Jesus even had a prayer life. I mean, can your mind fathom that? Jesus, the son of God, having a prayer life?! It not only blows my mind, but it always eliminates my excuse for not taking the time to have a prayer life for myself. It is imperative to our Christian walk that we stay connected to our heavenly father through prayer. Our prayer today should be one of thanks. We should thank God for his availability to us and for his desire for us to connect with him on a more intimate level. God is so good and has been so good to us, the least we can do is have a conversation with him. I promise you, once you start talking to him, you're going to love the end results.

Pray with me:

Lord, I thank you for this day. I ask that you forgive me for my sins, those that I know of and those that I do not. Father, I just want to take the time to say thank you. Thank you for your patience, for your love, for your kindness, for your mercy, and for your grace. I also want to thank you for always being available to me, even when I don't always make myself available to you. You have always been here, patiently waiting for me to meet with you. So, father, I thank you for the opportunity today to come before you and I pray that a fire is lit inside of me to come to you every day because you deserve my undivided attention. I thank you in advance for hearing my prayer. In Jesus' name, AMEN.

Good morning God activity page

What have you learned?

How often do you communicate with God?

What are some ways in which you can spend more time with God more?

I'm angry

Read; Proverbs 15:18; Ephesians 4:6

As human beings, we are driven by a number of emotions. Fear can keep us bound. Jealousy will have you walking around in a constant state of insecurity. Happiness has the ability to make you smile, even when no one else around you is smiling. At times, we all can be some really emotional people. Being emotional does not mean being a cry baby. It means being overwhelmed by one emotion in particular or a collection of emotions. Why am I talking about emotions you ask? I am trying to set the stage for one of the most controversial emotions that we have, and that is; anger.

Over the years I have encountered many people that deal with this particular emotion and I have learned that we all interpret anger to be many different things. Some think that using foul language and fighting is a result of being angry, while others may think that wanting to be alone because someone offends them, is a result of being angry. Whatever you do, and however you interpret this emotion, one thing is for sure; we are not to let it consume us, cause us to sin, or even go to bed with it. Anger can be complex but it can also be a blessing.

The scriptures today simply tell us to be slow to anger. What in the world does that even mean? When one is slow to anger, that means that this person has their emotions in check and has the ability to let something bother them, but not to the point where they will have a negative response that will result in sin. Did you know that anger is a God-given emotion? God knew that people were going to wrack our nerves and wrong us from time to time. Think about Jesus. He is the prime example of being wronged, yet the ultimate example of love and kindness. How can we do this? How can we come face to face with anger and choose to respond in love? It's not easy, but it is necessary to our Christian walk. The best answer that I have is to perhaps take a step back and examine what has us angry in the first place. Then we need to gauge our responses to the anger. It is not the anger that messes us up, it is how we respond when we are angry that can put us on the road to destruction. I am not only speaking of physical destruction but emotional destruction as well.

Let our prayer today be one that focuses on controlling this particular emotion, and not letting it consume us. We have the ability to gauge how angry we get, and the power to not give in to what can be the catastrophic results of our anger. Let us go before our father, to simply help us keep our emotions in check, even though sometimes we just really want to pop off.

Pray with me:

· Lord, I thank you for this day. I ask that you forgive me for my sins, those that I know of and those that I do not. Father, I ask that you help me with all the different emotions that come my way, that may play into me not being able to control my anger. I ask that you remove any and everything that is not like you, and show me how to be a better thinker, not only for my sake but for the sake of those who choose to be around me. I thank you in advance for hearing my prayer. In Jesus' name, AMEN.

Good morning God activity page

What have you learned?

Name a time when your anger got out of hand?

Looking back, what could you have done to change the outcome?

Tearing some stuff up

Read; Luke 5:17-25

What kind of friends do you have? Are they the kind that cosigns with you no matter what? Or are they the kind that will tell you when you are wrong then take you out to lunch later? As well-balanced humans, we have to have a support system around us. We simply cannot just go through life without the help, and encouragement of others. Picking our friends is just as important as picking out a good doctor, or a healthy meal to sustain us for the day. If we choose wrong, we can end up hurt and broken, but if we choose right, we could end up with lifelong companionship that promotes a healthy spiritual life, physical health, and even mental health.

The scripture for today is a really good one. Here, we have a group of friends with one friend who has a problem. The man could not walk. Jesus just so happened to be at someone's house teaching and sharing the gospel. The man and his friends decided that they wanted to pay a visit to Jesus so that he could heal their crippled friend. Scripture does not indicate how far they carried this man on his bed to their final destination, but it does say that when they arrived, the house was so packed that they could not get into the front door. What did these friends decide to do? They decided to climb the roof of someone else's home and tear a hole in the ceiling big enough to lower the man down right in front of Jesus. WOW! I mean, really? Do you have friends like this? Friends that are not only willing to carry you through the trenches but also willing to tear some stuff up in order for you to get what you need? This man had some bold friends. They loved him enough to physically carry him to his destination and were spiritually crazy enough to believe that Jesus was going to heal him. I encourage you today to ask God to place healthy people in your life that are going to encourage you, uplift you, and most of all, pray for and with you, trusting that God is going to do just what he said.

Pray with me:

Lord, I thank you for this day. I ask that you forgive me for my sins, those that I know of and those that I do not. God, I ask that you put people around me and in my path that are bold like the paralyzed man's friends. Lord, I want friends that are going to not only be there for me physically but also have that crazy child-like faith that will cause them to tear some stuff up, just to get to you, on my behalf. Lord, help me to be that kind of a friend. Let me be able to stand in the gap and go above and beyond the call of duty in order to get a friend who is in need, before your feet. I thank you for this day and I thank you that you have heard my prayer in advance. In Jesus' name, AMEN.

Good morning God activity page

What have you learned?

_____

_____

_____

_____

_____

_____

_____

_____

_____

_____

Make a list of all your friends who would "tear some stuff up" for you.

What type of people do you desire God to place in your life?

What can't he do?

Read; Numbers 11:23

I want you to think about this question that is getting ready to be asked, and be honest with your answer. When you get into a bind, what is the first thing your mind goes to? Does a financial bind cause you to think about borrowing from someone, or taking out some kind of loan? Does a physical condition cause you to immediately think about finding a physician to help you with your problem? What are your initial thoughts? I'll tell you a story about myself.

One day last year, I woke up in the middle of the night with a pain that shot through my neck. In my mind, I'm thinking that I might have pulled a muscle or something. I got up and walked around for a minute then laid back down. The pain was still present. As I am lying in the bed, my mind is going through my mental catalog of doctors that I might need to call to see what is going on. I go on with my thoughts for about a good 15 minutes before the Lord speaks to me. He asked, "What do you do when you wake up with a problem that you did not go to bed with"? I immediately repented and started praying about my situation. My first thoughts were not to pray and ask God to touch my body, but instead, they were trying to find a doctor. Mind you, the pain was not that severe and it was 3:00 in the morning. I encourage those who are in a severe situation to not only pray but to seek medical help. Please, do not be ignorant of the resources that God has out there for us. Anyway, back to the story. I began to pray for the lord to touch my body. I was able to go back to sleep. I woke up later that morning feeling much better and was able to go to work. That night it happened again. My husband insisted that we go to the emergency room. Long story short, I found out that I had a pulmonary embolism (blood clot in the lung) in my right lobe. I was terrified. I was all alone in the ER. Due to COVID, my husband could not be inside with me, and that made my fear even worse. While waiting in the car, however, he called on our ministry family to pray for me as well as my blood family. The scripture reading today reminded me of such a scary time in my life.

In order to understand this verse, we have to back up a bit and see what led to God's question and statement. The children of Israel were out in the wilderness and were growing tired of all the manna that God had been providing. They wanted more. They wanted meat. God says sure. Not only will I give you flesh, but I will give it to you for a whole month. You will have so much of it until it starts to come out of your nostrils and become loathsome to you. (They did a lot of complaining) Moses wanted to know how God was going to provide so much meat for so many people. He asked God if the flocks and the herds would be slain. Then God, with all of his awesomeness, responds in verse 23. God simply asked him, "Do I not have the ability to save you?" I love this response. It literally gives me chills. While Moses and even ourselves are sitting here worried about the HOW, we forget about the WHO.

In my personal story, my mind initially went to a doctor, when my natural instinct should have been to take it to my father. I may not have questioned God, as Moses did, but my mentality sure didn't trust him enough to consider him first. We have to train ourselves to allow God to be the first point of contact when a situation arises. God's hands are not short. He has the ability to give us what we need. The quicker we are able to understand verse 23, then the sooner we are able to let our father be our first call when a problem is present. Let this be our prayer today.

Pray with me:

Lord, I thank you for this day. I ask that you forgive me for my sins, those that I know of and those that I do not. Father, I thank you that you have an abundance of resources to give us just what we need when we need them. I ask that you help me to call on you first when I have a dilemma and to understand that there is nothing that you can't do and that you don't need any of MY resources to do it. You can and you will provide for me and my family all by yourself. I thank you for this day and I thank you that you have heard my prayer in advance. In Jesus' name, AMEN.

Good morning God activity page

What have you learned?

Has there been a time when God provided for you with his resources and not yours? Explain.

Reflect on a time when God should have been your first point of contact.

Let us pray

Read; Luke 11:1

I know, I know. Here I go again with a message about prayer. We can never talk about prayer enough. It is essential to being a Christian. We must have a prayer life. How can you be a child of God, but never take the time to talk to God? Not only are we supposed to be praying and speaking to God, but we are also supposed to be taking the time to be still and listen to him as well. How many of us can honestly say that when we are done praying, we sit a while to hear if God has a response? I will be honest and say that I have been guilty of this very action. There have been countless times where I have prayed and gotten up without waiting to see if my father had anything to add. I do understand that some people feel as if God doesn't speak to them, and that's okay. I promise that he is communicating with you in some capacity, but since it's not in the way that we expect, we can't recognize that it is him a lot of times. If you are not sure, tell him! There is absolutely nothing we can't run by God! Tell him how you are feeling and what you need from him. Then watch him show up and show out.

I chose this scripture for today for a particular reason. When I was getting ready to read this chapter and get this profound word concerning prayer, I came to a standstill with verse one. After reading it, I was hit with a question. Of all the things the disciples could have asked Jesus, why did they ask for him to teach them how to pray? At this point, Jesus had performed some mighty miracles and had preached and taught some mighty words. The disciples had been a witness to it all, but they chose to ask him to teach them how to pray. Why? I think that they figured out that prayer was connected to all of the things that they had seen Jesus do. Jesus was always in prayer. There are quite a few times in the bible where we see him go off to pray and this did not go unnoticed by those that were around him. Jesus taught them, and us, how important it was to stay connected to God our father no matter what, simply by his actions.

In the chapter we see Jesus explain to the disciples in what manner they should pray and how to address God. Christ knew the importance of staying in constant connection with our source and he was relaying this message through his actions, for all of us to see. If I have said it once, I have said it a million times before, GET A PRAYER LIFE! If Jesus Christ himself had one, what makes you think that you don't need one?

Pray with me:

Lord, I thank you for this day. I ask that you forgive me for my sins, those that I know of and those that I do not. Father, I ask that you show me how to address you in a manner that is pleasing. I know that it is imperative to my Christian walk to stay connected to you lord, but it is not always so easy. So, father, I ask that you highlight those distractions that are around me, so that I may be able to see them and rid myself of them. I do not want anything or anybody hindering me from being able to connect with you. You are my Lifesource and I need you to survive. I thank you for this day and I thank you that you have heard my prayer in advance. In Jesus' name, AMEN.

Good morning God activity page

What have you learned?

_____
_____
_____
_____
_____
_____
_____

How often do you pray?

_____
_____
_____
_____
_____
_____
_____
_____
_____

What are some ways that you can incorporate prayer into your life more?

_____
_____
_____
_____
_____
_____
_____
_____
_____

First thing first

Read; Psalm 118:24

Think fast! What is the first thing you do when you wake up in the morning? Do you turn on the television, grab your phone, or just simply start your day? Who is the first person that you speak to? Is it your spouse, the kids, the dog? Last question; what is the first emotion that you seem to feel when you wake up? Do you feel joy, anxiety, anger? What does this have to do with the scripture for today? The answer is very easy...everything.

We have to remember that every day belongs to the lord. He saw fit to wake us up, even when he didn't have to. Even when we do not deserve it. How do we repay him for this precious gift called life? We start off our day without acknowledging him. We choose to grab our phones rather than our bible. We allow emotions to overtake us instead of going into prayer. It is important for us to remember that this is indeed a day that the Lord has made, and no matter what, we are to rejoice and be glad in it. Let's try starting our day off by acknowledging him.

When we can totally understand that he should be our first point of contact, it will be easier to see this scripture for its worth. I translate this scripture as not only acknowledging that God created this day and that we should be happy, but I also translate it as, God has created this day for us to rejoice and be glad, but we can't do that if he is not at the beginning, middle, and end of our day. How can we be joyful when we don't have God at the center of our joy? Let our prayer today be one that acknowledges the goodness of our God.

Pray with me:

Lord, I thank you for this day. I ask that you forgive me for my sins, those that I know of and those that I do not. Father, I want you to be my first point of contact when I wake up in the morning. I want to be able to truly say that this is a day that you have made and that I will rejoice and be glad in it, no matter what comes my way today. I recognize that the only way that this will happen is if I keep you first throughout my day. You are an awesome God and there is absolutely none like you. I give you all the honor, all of the praise, and all of the glory, this morning. I thank you for this day and I thank you that you have heard my prayer in advance. In Jesus' name, AMEN.

Good morning God activity page

What have you learned?

_____
_____
_____
_____
_____
_____
_____
_____
_____
_____

What is the first thing that you do in the morning?

_____
_____
_____
_____
_____

What does the scripture Psalms 118:24 mean to you?

That hasn't even happened yet

Read; Exodus 4:1

How many of you have stressed over something that hasn't even happened? It is so easy for us to assume that something is going to be one way, that we can't even consider it turning out another way. When we do this, the good thing becomes ineligible, because we have automatically prepared ourselves for the worse. There is a famous quote by Muhammad Ali Jinnah that often gets repeated on a regular basis. It says; "Expect the best, prepare for the worst." I have even repeated this and have tried to live by it as well. With God though, do we really have to prepare for the worst? Our God opens doors that no man can close, and he closes doors that no man can open. So, if it is for me, it is for me, and if it is not for me, that doesn't mean that it is the worst. It's God saying, "not right now." It is so easy for us to brace ourselves for a negative outcome, but let's try a different approach. Why don't we try putting our faith, that we claim to have, in God and allow him to see us through?

The scripture for today is a bit of an odd one. In the chapter prior, God has appeared to Moses in the burning bush. In so many words, God tells Moses that he will be the one that he uses to deliver the children of Israel out of Egypt. God tells him what to do and even what to say. But the first verse in chapter four shows Moses disqualifying himself.

He tells God that the children of Israel will not believe him, nor will they believe that the Lord had appeared to him.

In my mind, I would like to think that if the Lord himself told me something, then I can hang my hat on that. Reality is, however, that God is always revealing promises to us in his word and we still choose to disqualify ourselves. When the word says that we are more than conquerors, we convince ourselves that we are not good enough. Let our prayer be today that we do not count ourselves out. If God says it, then it is so. No matter how we think or feel about it.

Pray with me:

Lord, I thank you for this day. I ask that you forgive me for my sins, those that I know of and those that I do not. Lord teach me how to not count myself out. I want to always know that whatever you say, and whatever you do, is always for my good. I thank you that my steps are already ordered and that your plan for me has already been written. I thank you for this day and I thank you that you have heard my prayer in advance. In Jesus' name, AMEN.

Good morning God activity page

What have you learned?

Name a time when you disqualified yourself?

What are some things you can do to help assure yourself that God is who he says he is?

Make it make sense Lord

Read; 2 Kings 4:1-7

God is awesome. In fact, he is so awesome, that sometimes his blessings don't even make sense. I won't give a prologue today because this story is amazing. Let's just dive right in.

Christian people! Christian people! What do you do when you are faced with a problem? In this story, this woman was married to a prophet who passed away. Her husband was a man of the lord. He died, leaving her with two sons and a massive amount of debt to deal with. She could see no way out. The creditor in which her husband owed wanted her sons in exchange for the debt. They would become slaves as payment. Of course, as a mother, she didn't want that to happen but also losing her sons meant losing her way of life. It does not share how old she was, or if she even had an occupation. In the Old Testament, women worked primarily in the home. So it can be assumed that without her sons, she would not be able to live like she had when her husband was alive. So, she was faced with losing her children and her livelihood.

She goes to the prophet Elisha and tells him of her situation. He asks her what she has in her house and she says that she has a pot of oil. He then tells her to go and borrow some empty vessels. Not only does he tell her to go borrow some, but he also instructs her to not borrow a few! Get this; she is already in debt and about to lose her kids. Now this man of God wants her to get deeper in debt? This doesn't make any sense at all. She, however, obeys the man of God's instructions to borrow the vessels and pours the oil that she already had into the empty vessels that she borrowed. God multiplied what she had and she was able to fill each vessel, sell off the extra oil, pay the creditor, keep her sons, and live out her days in peace. God! Make it make sense! What kind of God do we serve that will provide for us in such a way as this?

Just like this widow, God will use what we have to give us what we need. It seemed like all was lost for this woman. She could have said no to borrowing the vessels. Who would have blamed her? She was already in enough debt. But she chose to listen to the man of God and was rewarded in such a mighty way.

I love this story because the blessing of God does not have to make sense to us. We just have to trust the process. Let our prayer today be not only one of thanks but also one that requests God to enrich our lives in a way that doesn't even make sense. So much so that others are blessed from the overflow.

Pray with me:

Lord, I thank you for this day. I ask that you forgive me for my sins, those that I know of and those that I do not. God, I thank you that your blessings don't have to make sense. I thank you that you love me enough to uniquely bless me in a way that is specially designed just for me. I thank you for multiplying what I have. I ask that you continue to be with me throughout this day, and continue to do what doesn't make sense to me, in my life. I thank you for this day and I thank you that you have heard my prayer in advance. In Jesus' name, AMEN.

Good morning God activity page

What have you learned?

Name a time when God provided for you and it didnt make sense?

What are some ways in which you can begin to trust God's process or strengthen your trust in his process?

In the flesh

Read; Matthew 4:1-11

We are some weak individuals. Let me rephrase that. Without God, we are some weak individuals. This flesh is faulty. Is it possible to beat it into submission? Absolutely! Is it easy? Absolutely not! There is nothing easy about going against the flesh. It is downright impossible to do if we are not holding on to the Lord and his word. What are you fighting daily? Is it winning, or are you fighting back with the power of the Holy Spirit?

In today's scriptures, we see Jesus being led out into the wilderness by the Holy Spirit. First off, this tells me that every dry place that I am in is not of the devil. There are some lessons that God wants us to learn out in the wilderness. Testimonies are created in the wilderness. While Jesus is in the wilderness, satan himself comes along and begins to tempt Jesus with a desire of the flesh. Jesus had just come off a forty-day fast. He was indeed hungry. Eating was not a problem. It was the manner in which satan wanted Jesus to satisfy the flesh. He wanted Christ to use his power to turn stone into bread just to appease his flesh. What "quick fixes" do we do to appease our flesh? How many times has it gotten you in trouble?

Satan then showed Jesus all the kingdoms of the world and offered them to him. We already know that Christ came to save the world. So, what was satan trying to do? I remember my pastor teaching that satan was trying to give Christ a way out from dying on the cross. How many of us have a mission and try to find easier ways to get to the end?

Was the detour worth it? Or does it end up messing up what we originally planned? What if Christ would have taken the detour? I shudder to think where we would be.

Finally, satan takes Jesus to Jerusalem on a pinnacle of the temple and tells Jesus to jump. He even had the nerve to attempt to throw scripture at him. Jesus responds and tells him that the word of God says to not tempt the Lord thy God.

Out of all this, I will tell you where my mind went. I wanted to know, how in the world satan had the gall to tempt Jesus Christ, the son of the living God? Then it hit me; satan is well aware of how weak this flesh is? He knew that Jesus in heaven could not fail, but what about the one wrapped in this faulty flesh? Satan figured he could tempt Jesus because even the enemy knows that this flesh is weak and can cause the best of them to fall. Don't you see? Your enemy knows how to fight you. He knows just what weapons he needs to make you crumble and fall.

Let our prayer today be a petition to God to help us with this weak flesh. Let us ask the Lord for strength in order to stand and resist when the enemy throws the things we love, but mean us no good, our way.

Pray with me:

Lord, I thank you for this day. I ask that you forgive me for my sins, those that I know of and those that I do not. God, I need help. My flesh is weak, and I am not always able to stand against the temptations that the enemy throws my way. I do, however, know that in your strength, and your strength alone, that I am able to resist him so that he may flee, just like your word says. I know that I can lean on you and I thank you for holding me up and loving me, even when it is not always deserved. I thank you for this day and I thank you that you have heard my prayer in advance. In Jesus' name, AMEN.

Good morning God activity page

What have you learned?

_____
_____
_____
_____
_____
_____
_____
_____
_____
_____

What "quick-fixes" have you done to appease your flesh?

_____
_____
_____
_____
_____
_____
_____
_____
_____
_____

How many times has it gotten you into trouble? Explain.

_____
_____
_____
_____
_____

Didn't I tell you not to do that?

Read; Genesis 3:1-6

How many of you have children? How many of you get annoyed when they do something you told them not to do? Let's flip it a bit; who remembers themselves being told not to do something by your parents or guardians, and yet did it anyway? My dad used to ask me;" what was I thinking?" when I would get into trouble. My response was that I wasn't thinking. Truth is; I was though. When we do something wrong and have to answer for our actions, our response shouldn't be that we weren't thinking. We, in fact, were thinking. Just not about doing the right thing.

Today's scripture is a familiar one. We have a lot of nerve judging Eve when we have been guilty of the same crime. Satan is slick. He hit Eve with good old-fashioned reverse psychology. She and Adam had clear instructions on what not to do and satan came along and formulated doubt in her mind. He begins to question her about what God really said in order to make her believe that she might have heard or understood wrong. I could also see where he could have possibly tried to set a stage for Eve to believe that maybe God was too strict. He beat all around the mulberry bush instead of arriving at the truth, and in the end, the doubt that began to formulate in her mind won the battle. She sinned, then offered Adam to be a part of the sin, and he participated as well.

God told them both not to do what they had done, but the enemy was right there to get her to question what God said. We can't say that they weren't thinking, because they were. Eve's thoughts shifted from thinking about what God said, to seeing herself biting that fruit to be like God. She began to desire it, and mentally she had already begun to revel in the expected conclusion of partaking of it. Don't we do the same thing? God tells us not to do something, but we do it anyway. Then, we have the nerve to judge Adam and Eve. We all have fallen victim to pleasing our own fleshly desires. It's not always so easy to resist at times, but we have to remember and remind ourselves of the consequences that follow behind our actions.

Let our prayer today be one that asks God to help us make good decisions, and that we are not easily influenced. Let us ask God to help us keep our focus on what is right. Remember, asking God is not enough though. We have to take action and make a conscious decision to think before we act.

Pray with me:

Lord, I thank you for this day. I ask that you forgive me for my sins, those that I know of and those that I do not. Father, I need your help. I do not always make the right decisions. Sometimes the result of that decision causes more strife in my life. Lord, I want to avoid the heartache, and make the right decisions, the first time around. Help me to clear my mind so that I may think before I act. Keep me today father and help me make good decisions. I thank you for this day and I thank you that you have heard my prayer in advance. In Jesus' name, AMEN.

Good morning God activity page

What have you learned?

Have you ever done something that God told you not to do? What happened?

What lesson did you learn from it?

Are you being led?

Read; Romans 8:14

At the very beginning of our marriage, we were low on funds. We were super young and still learning. I remember one day, in particular, I needed something. I had been stressed out about it. I prayed about the matter and went on about my morning. I ended up going to the store with my mother later that day and ran into my grandmother. She was a woman of God who absolutely loved the Lord. You are a blessed individual if you ever had the opportunity to cross her path. She was coming out of the store when I was going inside the same store. She smiled at me and came my way. I noticed that she had her hand cuffed into a ball and immediately I knew what she was about to do. (She had a habit of rolling up money in her hand and giving it to you with her fist balled up.) Her giving me the money was a blessing in itself, but the words that she spoke still sit with me to this very day. When she handed me the money, she said; "I heard you praying this morning." That was all she said. Nothing else. Then she walked away.

Fast forward to all these years later, and this encounter still rests with me. When I read Romans 8:14, I thought about my "Gram Bam" (my nickname for her), being led to bless me. How was she led though? How did she feel compelled? The answer is quite simple; she spent time with the Lord and he gave her the intel. When reflecting back on this time in my life, a question was posed to me. How many messages and blessings have we failed to deliver because of our inability to be in tune with the Holy Spirit? What intel were we privy to and chose not to obtain due to our actions of not reading our word, not praying to God, and not spending time with him? My granny was led because she listened. She was led because she spent time with the master. She was led because she was a daughter of God.

The scripture today says that we are the sons (and daughters) of God when we are led by him. When we allow someone to lead us, we are putting complete trust and confidence in their ability to get us to our final destination unscathed. That should be our attitude concerning God. Let us not miss our opportunity to bless the people God has lined up to receive from us, because we can't have a relationship with him and be led. We must walk into our full potential so that the people around us can walk in theirs.

Pray with me:

Lord, I thank you for this day. I ask that you forgive me for my sins, those that I know of and those that I do not. Father God, I ask that you show me how to follow your lead. Lord, I want to do what you have called me to do. This means that I need the distractions that may hinder me from spending time with you to be silenced. I do not want to miss out on any important information that you may have for me to know. Help me Lord, so that I may help not only myself but others as well. I thank you for this day and I thank you that you have heard my prayer in advance. In Jesus' name, AMEN.

Good morning God activity page

What have you learned?

_____

_____

_____

_____

_____

_____

Elaborate on a time when God led someone to bless you.

Have you ever been led to bless someone else? Explain

You always have a choice

Read; James 4:8

God gives us "free will" to make whatever choices we want to make concerning our lives. There is no light bulb that comes on, or a certain age that we get to that will determine that it is time to start living for God or even taking our walk more seriously. Even though God doesn't force our hand, he does make it next to impossible for us not to serve him. His love is so raw and so pure, that he never grows tired of opening his arms to us. Nothing we can do or say would be able to separate us from His unconditional, non-judgemental, unapologetic love.

Today's scripture is a simple text, but it packs a mean punch. It didn't start off by saying; clean yourself up and be perfect, then draw near to God. It just says to draw near to him and he will draw near to you. It just says to wash your sins and purify your hearts. We can't clean ourselves up. It's impossible. However, if we choose to draw to our father and follow his commandments, we can be cleansed through the blood of Jesus Christ.

Let our prayer today be one that asks God to help us with our spiritual walk. We often pray for material things, but do we ever pray for enhancement of our spiritual walk? Let's try that today. Let us also pray for those in our lives who need to make a choice to either draw to God or stay where they are. Maybe you are in that very same place, and that is okay. You can always come unto him. He is ready whenever you are. I would suggest that you not keep him waiting for too long, for your soul's sake.

Pray with me:

Lord, I thank you for this day. I ask that you forgive me for my sins, those that I know of and those that I do not. Father, I ask that you help me with this Christian journey. I do not have it all together. I am so grateful that you love me past my flaws and that there is nothing you wouldn't do for me. Lord, I ask that you keep me focused on you. Give me the ability to shut everyone and everything out, and only tune in to you and the will you have for me. I thank you for this day and I thank you that you have heard my prayer in advance. In Jesus' name, AMEN.

Good morning God activity page

What have you learned?

What are some things in your life that you need to "clean up"?

What steps will you take to draw closer to God?

Order of operations

One of the many things that I love about God is; that he makes sure to take care of his children thoroughly. When we ask Christ to come into our lives, we inherit benefits. To the world, these benefits are not clear, but to the "knowers"(we are more than just believers), they are as clear as crystal. One of the major benefits is eternal life. But this will not be the topic of discussion today.

In today's scripture, we see that Christ is talking. To sum it up, he is saying that we should not worry about what we are going to eat, how we are going to clothe ourselves, or even where we will lay our heads at night. All of these things are included in our heavenly benefit package. When we decide to follow Jesus, we open up the doors for things that we probably thought we were not entitled to. But God is forever faithful to provide, even when we are undeserving.

There are some things that we have to do, however. We can not let God do all the work while we sit back and do nothing. Verse 33 tells us to seek first the kingdom of God, and his righteousness, and all these things will be added unto us. This means we have steps to follow.

In math, there is something called "the order of operations". There are particular steps that have to be taken, and in a specific order, or the equation will not be solved correctly. I found out that God *also* has an order of operations and the first step is to seek him and his righteousness. There is no way that we can make sound decisions or travel through life without God leading the way. This is why we have to keep him at the forefront of our lives. Every day we should strive to seek and do his will and not our own.

Let our prayer today be a prayer that asks God to show us how to seek Him and His righteousness first. Let us pray that we make good decisions and that we are pleasing him so that we can fully take advantage of all the heavenly benefits that he has in store for us. I don't know about you, but I want to utilize my entire package.

Pray with me:

Lord, I thank you for this day. I ask that you forgive me for my sins, those that I know of and those that I do not. Father, I can admit to you that I need your guidance in seeking you first. It is not always easy, but I know that it is necessary. I desire a hunger and a thirst to know you, and to submit myself to your will while releasing my own. Thank you, Lord, for never growing tired of me, and for always carrying me through, even when I don't recognize it. I want everything that you have for me, God. And with you leading my path, I know that obtaining all my bottled-up blessings are just around the corner. I thank you for this day and I thank you that you have heard my prayer in advance. In Jesus' name, AMEN.

Good morning God activity page

What have you learned?

_____

_____

_____

_____

_____

_____

_____

_____

What doors do you need God to open up for you?

In what ways are you seeking him first?

Charging God foolishly

Read; Job 1:22

Have you ever been angry or upset with someone which caused you to speak out against them? Admit it, we all have taken part in shedding someone in a bad light. When we are crossed, or feel like we have been crossed by someone, it is in our human nature to either lash out at that person or speak ill of the situation to those in our innermost circle. A lot of people have taken it further and aired their grievances out on social media. (I'm sure none of you do that though). When we do that, we are shedding a bad light on an individual and are indeed saying that this person is someone totally different than what you may know. Words don't even have to be spoken at times, to get your point across concerning how you feel about a person either. All of these things can cause someone else to view that individual negatively.

Did you know, we can do the same thing to God when we are deep in our feelings? Today's text comes from the book of Job. We all know the story of Job and what he went through. I personally am not sure if I could have lived through it. However, despite all of the things that Job endured, the bible says that he did not charge God foolishly. But what does that even mean? Charging God foolishly simply means to attribute God to anything that is not consistent with his goodness and his wisdom. So when we don't keep his commandments and we are supposed to be Christian people, we are shedding God in a bad light. A lot of the time, we are the only "church" some people see, and the only bible they read. We can never be perfect, but we are not to be out here living a life that is contradictory to what the word of God says either. It confuses people. So many people have run away or have stayed away from the church because of so-called "church people" and their un-Christian-like ways. This is a form of charging God foolishly. Our attitudes and lifestyle can cause people to believe that God is the total opposite of who he actually is to those who don't know him at all.

So what am I saying? I am simply saying that we need to do better. Let our prayer today be that God highlights those things that are not like him that may cause us to unknowingly charge him foolishly. I don't ever want to shed a bad light on God because of something I said, or ever did. We should always strive to practice what we preach so that others will not turn away from us, but gravitate towards the light that is within us.

Pray with me:

Lord, I thank you for this day. I ask that you forgive me for my sins, those that I know of and those that I do not. Father, I ask that you shine a light on those things in my life that are not like you. I never want to be a hindrance to anyone, and never want to shed you in a negative light. I want people to see me and want the God that lives in me, to live inside of them as well. Forgive me if I have charged you foolishly, whether it was through my words or even my actions. I thank you for grace and your mercy and I thank you that you have heard my prayer in advance. In Jesus' name, AMEN.

Good morning God activity page

What have you learned?

Have you ever charged God foolishly? How?

What are some things that you need to change in order to be more effective in the kingdom of God?

Kill it

Read; Galatians 5:24

I don't know who in the world said that being a Christian was easy, but I promise you, they lied! It takes some serious work to be a Christian. We literally have to kill that old us. You know, that us that wants to go off on that person that swerved in front of us on the highway. Or that person that said something slick in the store. The old us would have probably said our peace in a not-so-Christian-like manner, but this new creature who we are supposed to be has to keep that tongue at bay. I will be the first to admit; it is not always easy to do the right thing and walk away. But if I don't want the Holy Spirit convicting me concerning my actions, and then making me go back to apologize, I guess I better do right the first time around.

Today's scripture is a simple one, but it means so much. We have to crucify this flesh. We can not fall victim to doing what our flesh wants us to. If we are children of God, we can not be led by our emotions. We must be led by the spirit. I said in a previous study that satan is very aware of how faulty this flesh is. He knows that without God, we are a weak bunch of people. He doesn't mind throwing things our way to see if we will give in. If we are not in the habit of trying to kill this flesh, we will fall victim each time.

Let our prayer today be a prayer that asks God to help us with this faulty flesh. To give us the strength to resist when we are pulled. We should be asking God for a 911 kind of help when it comes to this flesh.

It's strong, but it makes us weak. But God is stronger, and he is here to help us overcome it all.

Pray with me:

Lord, I thank you for this day. I ask that you forgive me for my sins, those that I know of and those that I do not. Father, I ask that you help me with this faulty flesh of mine. I can't do this alone. I need you to help me resist all the tricks that the enemy has for me. Show me what I need to do in order to kill this flesh. There is no way that any of this can be done without you. I want to walk closer to you and I can't do that if my falling victim to the flesh gets in the way. I thank you for this day and I thank you that you have heard my prayer in advance. In Jesus' name, AMEN.

Good morning God activity page

What have you learned?

_____

_____

_____

_____

_____

_____

_____

_____

_____

_____

What are some things in your life that you need crucified?

_____

_____

_____

_____

What are some steps that you can take to stay away from the things that are not of God?

Be thankful for it all

Read; 1 Thessalonians 5:18

At the very beginning of last year, I had a blood clot in my right lobe. That was so scary. As a 10+ year healthcare worker, blood clots have always been one of the things that I feared. They are sneaky. The big ones do major damage and the little ones break off and get into places they don't belong, and then do major damage. Fast forward to mid-year. I get COVID. The first two days I was really sick. On the third day, I felt pretty good. The days that followed were filled with fever, achy body, and being tired all the time. But honestly, nothing too major. It turned a little scary about 12 days in. My O2 saturation dropped to 89%. I will not lie and say that it didn't frighten me a bit, because it did. It also, however, put determination in me to push forward. Instead of going to the hospital, I went to my physician and received medication. I began to walk around the house as best as I could. It was hard and I didn't want to do it, but it was necessary to my healing. I walked, climbed the stairs, and walked some more. Each day I got stronger. It got to the point where I wasn't coughing up a lung anymore when I reached the top of the stairs. I was getting back to my old self. Why am I sharing this? Honestly, that wasn't the plan. God, however, didn't allow me to endure all that I have, only for me not to tell of his goodness. Someone needs to know.

The scripture today is important to me. It reminds us that no matter what we go through, as long as we have breath in our bodies, we must give thanks, because whatever we are going through has already been ordained. My illnesses, especially having COVID, opened up my eyes to some of the trivial stuff that I allowed to infiltrate my mind and my heart. All of it seems extremely petty in the grand scheme of things now, but I couldn't see that at the time. It took an illness to open my eyes, and I am thankful for it. God will allow lessons to be learned any way they can be. Am I saying God gave me this? No. But he allowed it. This did not take him by surprise. There was something that I needed to know. Even though my human self allows things to still creep up in me, I am able to reflect and then check myself. I am forever thankful to God for allowing me to go through something that will cause me to be a better version of myself. What I went through doesn't even touch the surface of what others went through so I won't pretend, but I will say that my story is mine. I can only state what I learned from my experience.

Let our prayer today be one of thanksgiving. Thanking God for all we have endured, because if you are reading this, it didn't kill you, and that is surely something to be thankful for.

Pray with me:

Lord, I thank you for this day. I ask that you forgive me for my sins, those that I know of and those that I do not. God, you are awesome. There is absolutely none like you. I am so thankful for everything that you have done. Waking me up this morning, letting me have use of all my limbs, and being in my right state of mind. Lord, you have always provided for me and my family and I know that you always will. Thank you for keeping me, even when I didn't know that I needed to be kept. You are an awesome God indeed. I give you all the praise, all the honor, and all of the glory in your mighty son Jesus' name. AMEN.

Good morning God activity page

What have you learned?

What are some battles you have faced?

How did you overcome these battles? How were you able to see God's glory in the midst?

Author's Note

Why Good Morning God?

Good Morning God was a thought years ago and only began to come about just a short while ago. I had gotten into the habit of waking up each morning so consumed with other thoughts, that the Lord was not on my mind at all. When I would wake up, I would look at my phone, deal with the kids or my husband, but I wouldn't even say good morning to God. After a while, God checked me about this. How is it possible to give energy to everything else first thing in the morning, and not even give reverence to the one that decided to breathe life into me today?

?*Good Morning God* is a collection of Bible-based messages that I was inspired to write and share with those who have decided to make God their first point of contact in the morning. They are quick, and to-the-point. I pray that they enhance your life and encourage you to put God before anything else. Let us all strive to put him at the top of our day, and see how better things will be for us.

I love you all. Be blessed.

T King

Journaling

Use these extra writing pages to jot down additional notes, or thoughts.

CPSIA information can be obtained
at www.ICGtesting.com
Printed in the USA
LVHW020933250222
711994LV00024B/1465